PIANO • VOCAL

the best of ANN HAMPTON CALLAWAY

6   At the Same Time

12 Blues in the Night

22 Come Take My Hand

19 How Deep Is the Ocean
    (How High Is the Sky)

28 How High the Moon

38 I Gaze in Your Eyes

48 I've Dreamed of You

43 If You Can't Sing It
    (You'll Have to Swing It)
    (a.k.a. Mr. Paganini)

52 My Buddy/Old Friend

59 The Nanny Named Fran

62 Perfect

66 A Quiet Thing

70 Twisted

76 Where Does Love Go?

84 You Can't Rush Spring

Photos: Bill Westmoreland

ISBN 0-634-08031-8

HAL•LEONARD® CORPORATION

7777 W. BLUEMOUND RD. P.O. BOX 13819 MILWAUKEE, WI 53213

Visit Hal Leonard Online at
www.halleonard.com

BIOGRAPHY

ANN HAMPTON CALLAWAY is one of the finest singer/songwriters of our time. The statuesque performer dazzles music lovers as a singer, pianist, composer, lyricist, arranger, actress and educator. Her talents have made her equally at home in jazz and pop as well as on stage, in the recording studio, on TV and in film. She is best known for starring in the hit Broadway musical *Swing!* and for writing and singing the theme to the internationally successful TV series "The Nanny." Ann is a devoted keeper-of-the-flame of the great American songbook. She brings fresh and original interpretations to these timeless classics and works to uphold the canon by writing songs with Cole Porter, Carole King, Barbara Carroll and others. Her spontaneity, intelligence and soulful charisma have won her a diverse fan-base including notables as Barbra Streisand, Clive Davis, Carly Simon and Wynton Marsalis.

The New York Times writes, "For sheer vocal beauty, no contemporary singer matches Ms. Callaway." Ann attributes her voice and love of music to her mother, Shirley, who throughout Ann's childhood sang and played torch songs, Gershwin and German lieder at the piano. Of the uniquely musical household she says, "I didn't know it at the time, but we were sort of the Von Trapp family of Chicago." After a music teacher discovered her unusually mature soprano voice, Ann was encouraged to study classically, honing the pitch-perfect control and expressive three-octave range she is known for. While her voice teachers suggested she could have a career in opera, Ann eventually realized that she would be happier singing the music she most loved. Inspired by Ella Fitzgerald, Sarah Vaughan, Frank Sinatra, Judy Garland, Joni Mitchell and Stevie Wonder, she was fascinated by the challenge of drawing these threads together into her own original singing style. After "serving two years" in college as an acting major, she packed her bags and moved to New York where she promptly got a job singing six hours a night at a piano bar. Her early days in New York caused a stir as she made a growing name for herself in watering holes and small cabarets throughout the city. She eventually became known as "the singer who stills the room." After receiving advice from legendary pianist and mentor George Shearing, she began stepping away from the piano and started performing with some of the finest musicians in jazz, refining her ability to scat, swing and inhabit a song. Today she travels with her musical director, Ted Rosenthal, who accompanies her in nightclubs and concert halls around the world. Her piano playing remains part of her performances as she concludes most concerts with her signature improvisation, playing and singing a hilarious and well-crafted song based on words and phrases called out from the audience.

Ann has become a favorite in the jazz and pops concert circuit, appearing as special guest artist with Wynton Marsalis and the Lincoln Center Jazz Orchestra and with Keith Lockhart and the Boston Pops at Symphony Hall and Tanglewood. She has sung with over twenty-five of the nation's top orchestras and big bands. Her performances in the Carnegie Hall tributes to Ella Fitzgerald, Peggy Lee and Harold Arlen were memorable and show-stopping. She performed for President Clinton in Washington, D.C. and was the invited guest performer for President Gorbachev's Youth Peace Summit in Moscow. Recently, she returned to Moscow for a sold-out engagement with Russian jazz star Igor Butman at Le Club. Ann performed with her sister, Broadway star Liz Callaway, in their award-winning show, *Sibling Revelry,* at London's Donmar Warehouse, and their recent show *Relative Harmony* has received rave notices. She performed with the BBC Big Band at the Edinburgh Festival in Scotland at The Queen's Hall for the Jubilee Celebration and had a highly successful concert tour throughout Australia and New Zealand. Ann has performed twice in Berlin's famed Philharmonie Hall by special invitation. She takes time out of her schedule to teach master classes during her travels, reaching out to a new generation of aspiring singers.

Ann recently signed with Telarc Records and is preparing to record her first CD for them, due in May of 2006. Ann's last CD, *Slow* (Shanachie Entertainment) garnered high critical acclaim and is her most emotionally revealing and pop-inspired album to date. Ann has recorded two popular holiday CD's—*Holiday Pops!* with Peter Nero and the Philly Pops and her solo CD, *This Christmas* (Angel/After 9). Her recording *Signature* (After 9) features the signature songs of the great jazz legends of the 20th century, performed with pianist Kenny Barron and guest artist Wynton Marsalis. Other CD recordings include *Easy Living* (After 9), *To Ella with Love* (After 9), *After Ours* (Denon), *Bring Back Romance* (DRG), *Ann Hampton Callaway* (DRG) and the award-winning live recording, *Sibling Revelry* (DRG). She has also been a guest artist on over forty CDs.

Ann fondly remembers the first song she made up at the age of three. But it wasn't until she first heard Carole King's *Tapestry* that she decided to devote herself to songwriting. Since then she has composed over 250 songs for television, Broadway, off-Broadway and several of today's leading interpreters of songs. Her music and lyrics have been performed and recorded by Barbra Streisand, Liza Minnelli, Patti Lupone, Michael Feinstein, Blossom Dearie, Peter Nero, Karrin Allyson, Donna McKechnie, Harvey Fierstein, Lillias White, Barbara Carroll, Amanda McBroom, Liz Callaway and Carole King herself. One of Ann's songwriting highlights was writing "Tonight You're All Mine" with Ms. King in the studio the same day it was recorded for the CD *Slow*. Carole was so generous that she even produced the track and sang backup vocals.

Another milestone was composing "At the Same Time" for Barbra Streisand and having Ms. Streisand record the peace anthem ten years to the date she wrote it. That recording, *Higher Ground*, debuted nationally at #1, giving Ann her first of three platinum records. Ms. Streisand asked Ann to write lyrics to a Rolf Lovland melody, which she entitled "I've Dreamed of You." Ms. Streisand received the song three hours before she was getting married and sang the song to James Brolin at their wedding. She later recorded it for her CD, *A Love Like Ours*, released it as a single and selected it for *The Essential Barbra Streisand*. She performed both of these songs on her live double CD, *Timeless*, for which Ann also wrote patter by Barbra's request. Ms. Streisand later chose Ann's song "A Christmas Lullaby" for her holiday CD, *Christmas Memories*.

The Cole Porter Estate officially recognizes Ann Hampton Callaway as the only composer to have collaborated with Cole Porter, having set her music to his posthumously discovered lyric, "I Gaze in Your Eyes." It was first recorded by Ann for Ben Bagley's *Cole Porter Revisited* series. Later, the song was recorded by Elaine Paige and was featured in the West End hit musical revue *A Swell Party*. Ann was one of the creators of the Broadway musical *Swing!*, writing the delightful "Two and Four" as well as several additional lyrics to the standards in the Tony®- and GRAMMY®-nominated score. In addition to the theme for "The Nanny," she has written the TV themes for "Day's End," "Cabaret Beat" and "The Jim J and Tammy Fay Show." Ann composed incidental music for the David Weiner play, *Baltimore Star*. Her songwriting is administered by Williamson Music.

Ms. Callaway's performances have been seen on numerous TV shows including *The Today Show*, CNN's *Larry King Live*, *The Charlie Rose Show*, *The Oprah Winfrey Show*, *The Rosie O'Donnell Show* and *ABC News*. She starred in "Midnight Swing" for the PBS television special "Live from Lincoln Center" and was featured in another PBS special with Keith Lockhart and the Boston Pops. Last summer she performed two songs for the NBC special "Macy's Fourth of July Fireworks Spectacular" and has made two appearances on NBC's "Macy's Thanksgiving Day Parade." Her voice has been heard in numerous TV jingles and voiceovers including spots for Coca-Cola, Ethan Allen and State Farm. Ann has also done extensive broadcasting for Sirius Satellite Radio as a performer, DJ and interviewer. She is in discussion about hosting a TV talk/variety show for singers and singer-songwriters.

Ann's dream of working in film is being realized in several recent projects. She can be seen making her feature film debut opposite Angelina Jolie and Matt Damon in the new Robert DeNiro film *The Good Shepherd*, performing the standard "Come Rain or Come Shine." She recorded "Isn't It Romantic?" and "The Nearness of You" in Wayne Wong's *Last Holiday*, starring Queen Latifah. Both films will be released internationally in 2006. In 2004, Ann was featured in the role of Mrs. White in the award-winning film *Volare* for Jim Henson Productions, directed by Tamela D'Amico. Ann is currently writing songs for the upcoming movie musical *State of Affairs*, directed by Philip McKinley.

Ms. Callaway's honors include receiving a Tony® Award nomination for Best Featured Actress in a Musical for her work in *Swing!*, and winning the Theatre World Award for Outstanding Broadway Debut. She has garnered an unsurpassed fourteen awards from The Manhattan Association of Cabarets and Clubs, two Backstage Bistro Awards, The 2005 Nightlife Award, The Johnny Mercer Songwriter Award and The Norman Vincent Peale Award for Positive Thinking.

Ann devotes much of her time to philanthropic causes, both as a singer performing in numerous benefits, and as a songwriter composing songs in times of need. In September 2005, Ann performed her original composition "Let the Saints Come Marching," written to honor Hurricane Katrina victims, on a national TV broadcast on the Fox News Channel. Her song "Who Can See the Blue the Same Again?" was released earlier in 2005 as a single, paying tribute to the tsunami survivors and raising much-needed money for The Tsunami Fund of The PRASAD Project. In the aftermath of September

11th, Ann composed the stirring anthem, "I Believe in America," which she performed on *Larry King Live* and released as a CD single. Just days after the tragedy, Ann heard an 8,000-year-old prayer from the Rig Veda and composed the world-renowned "Let Us Be United." Ann recorded the song with Kenny Werner, The Siddha Yoga International Choir and five-year-old Sonali Beaven, who sang in honor of her father who lost his life on Flight 93. It was released on CD and DVD and its proceeds continue to benefit Save the Children and The PRASAD Project.

Ann's father is John Callaway, Chicago's legendary TV and radio journalist, and an acclaimed author, moderator and speaker. Her mother, Shirley Callaway, a superb singer, pianist and one of New York's most in-demand vocal coaches, was recently featured at New York's Town Hall, singing with Ann and her sister, Liz. Ann resides in New York. She lives by the creed best expressed in the Andre Gide quote: "Art is the collaboration between God and the artist and the less the artist does, the better."

◆

For more information, visit her website at **www.annhamptoncallaway.com.**

AT THE SAME TIME

Words and Music by
ANN HAMPTON CALLAWAY

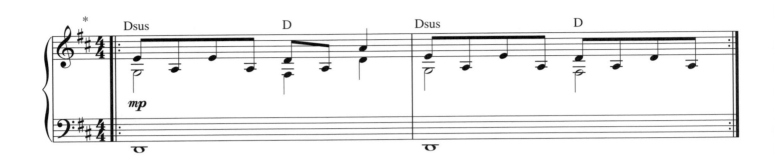

Think of all ___ the hearts ___ beat - ing in the world ___ at the
Think of all ___ the chil - dren be - ing born in - to this world ___ at the
Think of all ___ the love ___ pour - ing from our hearts ___ at the

same time. ___
same time. ___
same time. ___

*Recorded a half step lower.

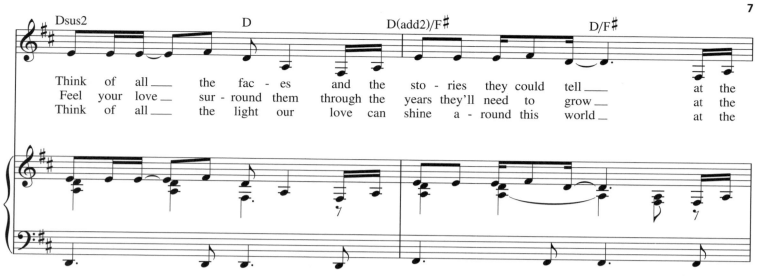

Think of all ___ the fac - es and the sto - ries they could tell ___ at the
Feel your love ___ sur - round them through the years they'll need to grow ___ at the
Think of all ___ the light our love can shine a - round this world ___ at the

same time. ___
same time. ___
same time. ___

Think of all ___ the eyes _____ look-ing out ___ in - to ___ this world, __
Think of all ___ the hands ___ that will be reach - ing for ___ a dream. __
Think what we've ___ been giv - en and then think what we ___ could lose. __

BLUES IN THE NIGHT
(My Mama Done Tol' Me)

Words by JOHNNY MERCER
Music by HAROLD ARLEN

Blues tempo

softly-as an echo

ma-ma done tol' me ___ when I was in { knee - pants, ___ / pig - tails, ___ } my

ma-ma done tol' me, ___ { son! ___ / hon! ___ } A A

woman's a two face,___
man is a two face,___
a wor - ri - some thing who'll leave ya t' sing the

blues ___ in the night. (Hum) ___

My ma - ma was right, there's blues ___ in the night.

HOW DEEP IS THE OCEAN
(How High Is the Sky)

Words and Music by
IRVING BERLIN

times a day ___ do I think of you? ___

How man - y ros - es are sprin - kled with dew? ___

___ How far would I trav - el

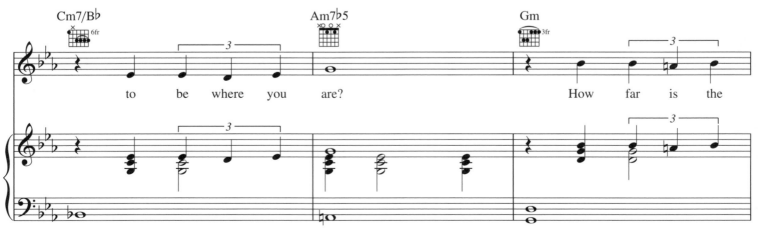

to be where you are? How far is the

COME TAKE MY HAND

Words and Music by
ANN HAMPTON CALLAWAY

Freely

Moderate Bossa

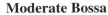

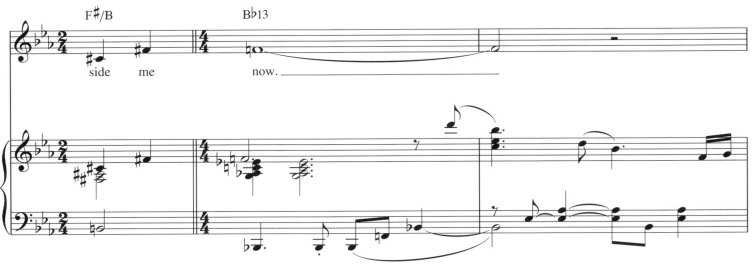

with all _____ our ___ love. ___

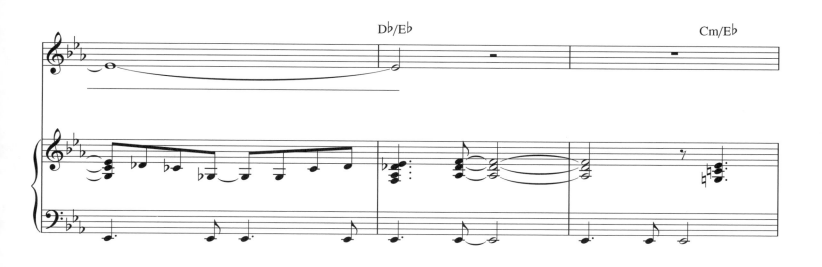

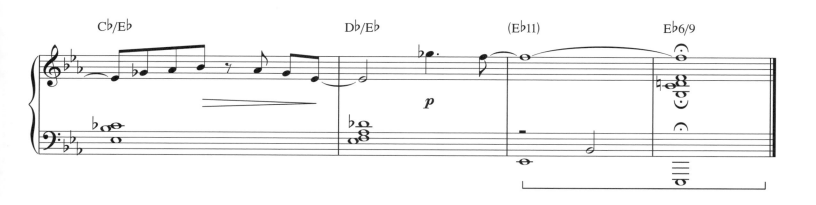

HOW HIGH THE MOON

Words by NANCY HAMILTON
Music by MORGAN LEWIS

Twice as fast

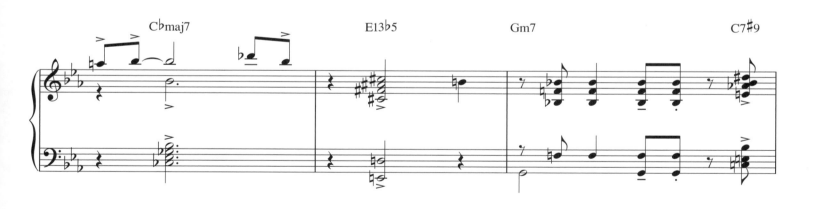

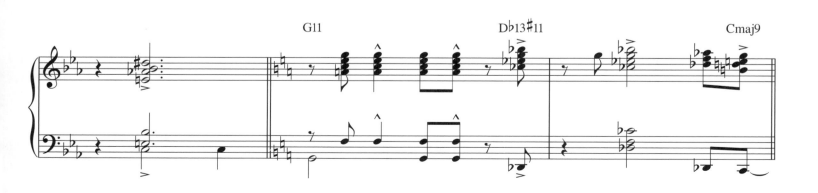

I GAZE IN YOUR EYES

Words by COLE PORTER
Music by ANN HAMPTON CALLAWAY

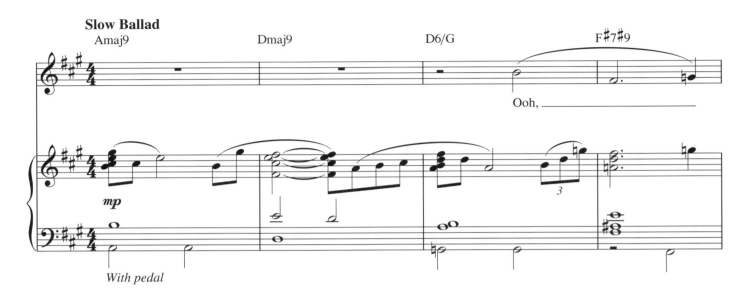

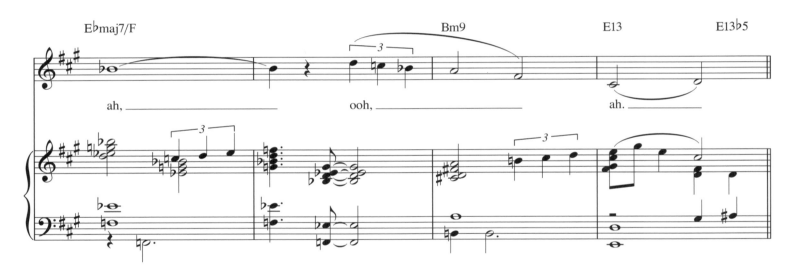

*Original lyric

IF YOU CAN'T SING IT
(You'll Have to Swing It)
(a.k.a. Mr. Paganini)

Words and Music by
SAM COSLOW

I'VE DREAMED OF YOU

Words and Music by ANN HAMPTON CALLAWAY
and ROLF LOVLAND

MY BUDDY/OLD FRIEND

MY BUDDY
Lyrics by GUS KAHN
Music by WALTER DONALDSON

OLD FRIEND

from I'M GETTING MY ACT TOGETHER AND TAKING IT ON THE ROAD

Lyrics by GRETCHEN CRYER
Music by NANCY FORD

Moderately slow, steady

THE NANNY NAMED FRAN

from the TV series THE NANNY

Words and Music by
ANN HAMPTON CALLAWAY

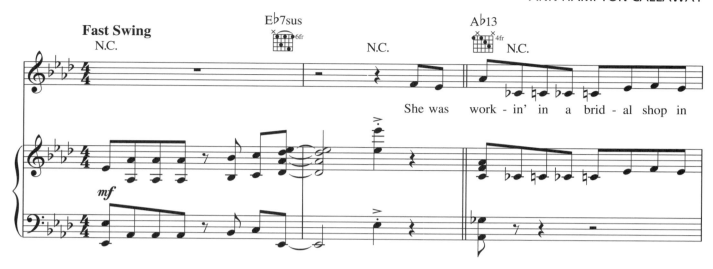

She was work-in' in a brid-al shop in

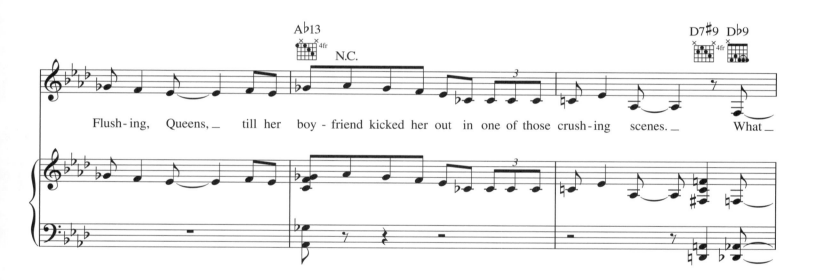

Flush-ing, Queens,___ till her boy-friend kicked her out in one of those crush-ing scenes.___ What___

___ was she to do? Where was she to go? She was out on her fan-ny!___

PERFECT

Words and Music by
ANN HAMPTON CALLAWAY

A QUIET THING

from FLORA, THE RED MENACE

Words by FRED EBB
Music by JOHN KANDER

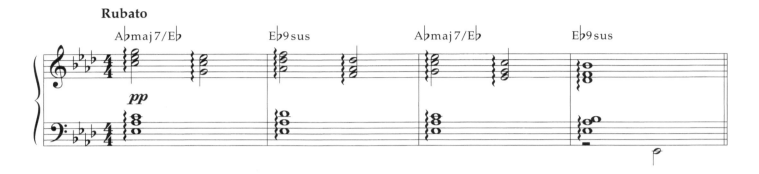

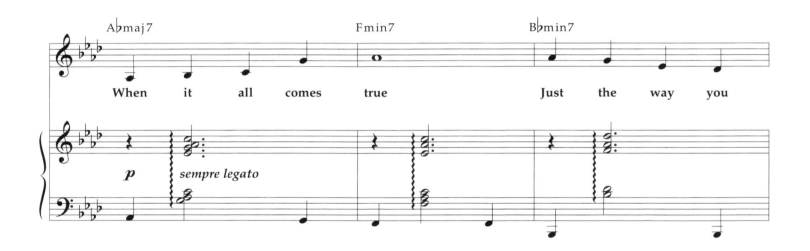

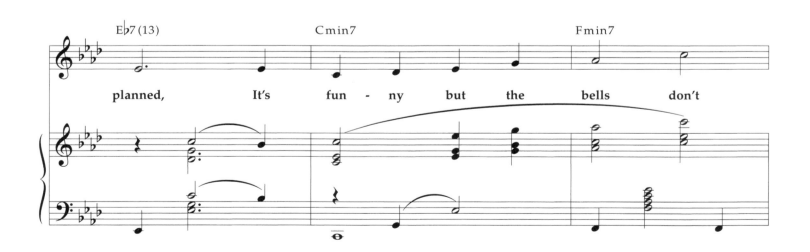

TWISTED

Words and Music by ANNIE ROSS
and WARDELL GRAY

WHERE DOES LOVE GO?

Words and Music by
ANN HAMPTON CALLAWAY

YOU CAN'T RUSH SPRING

Words and Music by
ANN HAMPTON CALLAWAY